Zen Of Watering™
Your Garden

Matthew M. Cohen M. D.

My Best
for continued
success in
the garden:

Pictures of B.o.d.
Campbell Irvine
on pages 19 & 21

Zen of Watering™ Your Garden
Matthew M. Cohen M. D.

www.zenofwatering.com   www.zofw.com

Copyright © 2007 Matthew M. Cohen M. D.

Library of Congress Control Number 2007906746

ISBN-13 978-0924381-25-6 (Softcover Edition)

Edited by Matthew M. Cohen M. D.

Text copyright © 2007 by Matthew M. Cohen M. D. except where noted
    in the Appendix of Contributing Authors
Photographs copyright © 2007 by Matthew M. Cohen M. D. except where noted
    in the Appendix of Contributing Photographers
Cover Design and Photographs by Matthew M. Cohen M. D.
Cover Title typestyle Viner ITC©

Published by SUNBELT PUBLISHERS
www.sunbeltpublishers.com
                    Division of Sunbelt Medical Publishers
            P.O. Box 13512
            Tallahassee, FL 32317-3512

**SUNBELT
MEDICAL
PUBLISHERS**

FORWARD

I have gardened more than fifty years and spent thirty of those years as a family physician, both of which prepared me for creating this book. My goal is twofold. The first is to provide an experience which nurtures the reader's relationship with things that grow in the earth – and in the soul. To this end, I have spent many hours taking photos of growing things around me, and many more on the web searching out other gardener-photographers who were willing to let me share their photographs with you. What you see as you turn the pages are my favorites out of the thousands of photos I reviewed for this book. I hope these alone make it a joyful experience for you.

My second goal is to inspire my readers to engage the garden in its own integrity and power. I use aphorisms, poetry, and other insightful observations – most found and some original – as companions to the plants in the photographs and as guides to the reader. As you will see, the arrangement of the pages is designed to create this relationship between words and pictures in the reader's mind. I encourage you to seek out and add your own companionable words as well.

Though I cannot claim to be a serious student of Zen, I chose to title my book The Zen of Watering Your Garden. For this, I owe a debt of gratitude to the writer Natalie Goldberg, who gave me the tools to recognize and name my own experience of encountering the garden. In much of her writing, Goldberg invites the reader to share her journey of awakening through the teachings and practice of Zen Buddhism. I was particularly instructed and inspired by her book Long Quiet Highway: Waking Up In America (1994), for through it, I came to understand the integral nature of a Zen experience and to recognize the Zen-like experiences I have been having over the years, most frequently and joyously in hand-watering the garden.

Other books have served to deepen these insights for me: Zen Seeing and Zen Drawing: Meditation in Action by Frederick Frack (1994), Zen and the Art of Motorcycle Maintenance by Robert J. Persig (1974) (which I read years ago), Zen Poems of China and Japan: the Crane's Bill compiled and translated by Lucien Stryk and Takashi Ikemoto (1994), and The Jew and the Lotus – A Poet's Rediscovery of Jewish Identity in Buddhist India by Rodger Kamenetz (1995). Many more can be found by the interested reader.

A bit of personal history may make my own journey more recognizable and instructive for the reader. In my medical practice and my frequently intense engagement with patients on their own life journeys, I became acutely aware of every person's need for periods of time to center the self, to reflect deeply, for time in which one can escape the troubled mind and relax into the present moment – in short, for those Zen or Zen-like experiences which keep the body whole, the mind calm, and the soul at peace. I learned from and with my patients that I, too, need such time for spiritual renewal.

In my own life, I have these experiences most often when hand-watering a plant, or my gardens, or even my lawn. I find myself avoiding the sprinklers so that I can hold the hose in my hand and let my mind flee those stressors common to a physician's and to everyone's life – life as a child's parent, a spouse's spouse, a needy friend's friend, a taxpayer to the government, a diligent and often weary worker, and other such unavoidable trials and tribulations. As I water, my thoughts clear and the weight falls from my shoulders. I feel my body and soul rejuvenate just like the plants I am sprinkling, and so become better able to do what needs to be done.

Yes, it sounds like a series of clichés, but if you are familiar with Goldberg's book, or are a Zen master or student, or practice meditation or contemplative prayer, then you too know the experience I am describing. Especially if you are a gardener, you know how often it is found in your garden. And in its fullest sense, of course, a garden can be anywhere that something grows and is cared for such as: an African violet on the desk, an orchid in the bay window, geraniums in the balcony box of the 7th floor apartment, tomatoes on the rooftop, roses in an 8x10' gated yard in the heart of New York, an acre of vegetables, fruits, and herbs to feed a family, perennials along the path and a patch of wild flowers in the corner of the yard, botanical gardens and parks in all the towns and cities of the world, and the soul. A plant, a collection of plants, a garden, many gardens, all offer an opportunity to retreat into the Zen of watering and through that into the serenity of the gardener's mind and spirit.

I hope this book can help you to connect with your own gardening – past and present – and inspire you to retreat often to the creating and nurturing of your gardens. I invite you to enter into the Zen of watering your gardens.

Matthew M. Cohen, M.D.

Dedicated to Gardeners Everywhere

Your home is your castle.

Your garden is your sanctuary.

Hand-watering brings you closer to nature

and

finding your inner-self and peace.

mmc

In all things of nature

There is something of

The marvelous.

Aristotle, (384-322 BCE)

14

Watering redirects your perception of the complex outside world. Being with the plants, with the garden cleansing and clarifying your inner self.

mmc

Watering the garden

Nourishes the plants and

Nourishes your body

Creating a haven for the mind.

mmc

18

Contemplating the garden

Is peaceful for your body

And a haven for the mind

And the soul.

                    mmc

20

All of him was gathered in this moment

and

concentrated on the

flower before him...

Natalie Goldberg of Dainin Katagari

Roshi, *Long Quiet Highway* 1993

22

This dewdrop universe

Just a dewdrop

And yet

And yet

      Kobiayashi Issa, (1763-1827)

24

Start your day watering by hand.

Allow your senses to rekindle your core.

Watch for surprises!

mmc

The rain comes when the wind calls.

Emerson, 1847, *Woodnotes II*

The branches bow; the bark stalls.

mmc

28

The years teach much which the days never knew.

Emerson, 1844, *Experience*

The Meaning of Life is to See.

Hui Neng, (638-713)

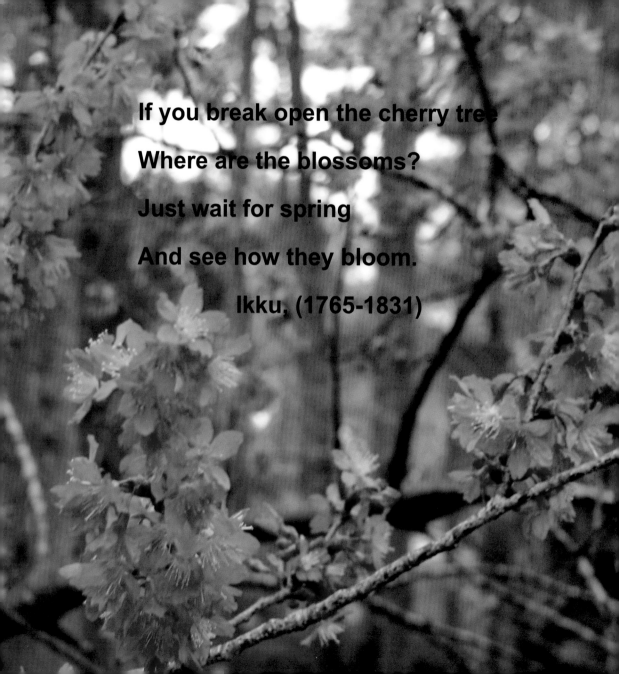

If you break open the cherry tree

Where are the blossoms?

Just wait for spring

And see how they bloom.

Ikku, (1765-1831)

Drops from the ancient hand pump

drip,

drip,

drip.

Ripples of life spread over time.

Mesmerizing

Where do they disappear?

They go to create new life.

mmc

Techniques pass from

generation to

generation.

The ancient spout

held by aged hand,

pours life

on the long-time companion.

mmc

36

The constant flow,

the source of life,

swiftly babbles through

the garden brook.

mmc

Conserve water and still
you have a special garden
and a special place.
                    mmc

The lonely little petunia

The lovely purple petunia

Who needs an onion patch!

mmc

Water sustains all.
Thales of Miletus, (624-547 BCE)

Seeking water,

sends life in different directions.

Leslie A. Slade, 2007

46

The garden is at rest, waiting for the morn,

All is sleeping peacefully, the roses and the thorn.

The sun jumps to life, to rise the wakeup call,

The bluebell rings its best, and the roses climb the wa

Rachel F. Blackman, 2007

Water, taken in moderation,

cannot hurt anybody.

Samuel Clemens aka Mark Twain

(1835-1910)

50

Water given in moderation

encourages healthy gardens.

mmc

If there is magic on the planet,

it is contained in the water.

Loren Eisely (1907-1977)

52

Floats by Chihuly

I would feel more optimistic about a bright future for man if he spent less time proving that he can outwit Nature and more time tasting her sweetness and respecting her seniority.

E. B. White (1899-1985)

Water is the driver

of Nature

da Vinci (1452-1519)

In the garden,

Autumn is,

indeed the crowning glory of the year,

bringing us the fruition of months

of thought and care and toil.

Rose G. Kingsley, 1905

58

Study nature,

love nature,

stay close to

nature. It will

never fail you.

Frank Lloyd Wright, (1867-1959)

Idyllic irrepressible nature

delights an individual's senses.

Imprinting indelibly.

Incredibly insinuating inward

ink-like impressions on

the soul.

                    mmc

Open, ready, and welcoming,

with water on their tongues,

they undulate through

the waves of ether

quenching their thirst.

                    mmc

Whatever is in any way beautiful has its source of beauty in

itself, and is complete in itself... Marcus Aurelius (121-180)

If gardeners will …

think of watering

as a matter of

"watering the earth"

under the plants…

The garden will get on very well.

Henry Beston,

Herbs and the Earth, 1935

68

**Spring passes and one remembers one's innocence
Summer passes and one remembers one's exuberance
Autumn passes and one remembers one's reverence**

Yoko Ono
Season of Glass
1981

Winter passes and one remembers ones's perserverance

There is nothing... as satisfactory or as thrilling, as gathering the vegetables one has grown.
Alice B. Toklas, 1954, *Alice B. Toklas Cook Book*

Nature does not hurry,

yet everything is

accomplished.

Lao Tzu (c. 6th Century BCE)

74

CALIFORNIA JUNIPER
donated by
Mas Moriguchi

Star Light, Star Bright,

Magenta Yellow and White

I wish I may,

I wish I might

Get the wish

I wish tonight.

modified nursery rhyme, mmc

I think that I shall never see
A poem lovely as a tree.

A tree whose hungry mouth is pressed
Against the earth's sweet flowing breast;

A tree that looks at God all day,
And lifts her leafy arms to pray;

A tree that may in summer wear
A nest of robins in her hair:

Upon whose bosom snow has lain;
Who intimately lives with rain.

Poems are made by fools like me,
But only God can make a tree.

Joyce Kilmer, 1917, Trees

Color in certain places

has the great value of

making the outlines and

structural planes seem more energetic.

Antonio Gaudi, (1852-1926)

82

Art is the unceasing effort to compete with the beauty of flowers -- and never succeeding
Mark Chagall, (1887-1985)

More than anything, I must have flowers, always, always.
Claude Monet, 1880

Which came first?
The chicken or the egg?

anonymous

The love of nature is a passion

for those in whom it once lodges.

It can never be quenched.

It cannot change. It is a furious, burning, physical

greed, as well as a state of mystical exaltation.

It will have its own way.

Mary Webb, 1920,

The House in Dormer Forest

90

A perfect beauty of a sunflower!

a perfect excellent lovely sunflower existence!

a sweet natural eye to the new hip moon, woke up

alive and excited grasping in the sunset shadow

sunrise golden monthly breeze!

Allen Ginsberg, 1955
from *Sunflower Sutra*

And far and wide, in a scarlet tide;

The poppy's bonfire spread.

Bayard Taylor, c 1880

All my life I have tried to pluck a thistle

and plant a flower

wherever the flower would grow

 in thought and mind.

Abraham Lincoln (1801-1865)

96

Leaves are verbs that conjugate the seasons.
Gretel Ehrlich, 1985, *The Solace of Open Spaces*

Watering, drooping leaves become alive,

Colorful petals awake and thrive.

Sponging roots absorb and flourish

For the many seasons they will nourish.

Stanley L. Cohen 2007

100

The secret of the receptive

Must be sought in stillness

Within stillness there remains

The potential for action.

Sun Bu-er, (c.1124-1182)

102

Windowsills are a perfect place for potted posies!
Naomi Matthews, 2007
©2007 Hillclimb Media.

Nature, like man, sometimes weeps for gladness.

Benjamin Disraeli, (1804-1881)

106

Fruits that blossom first will first be ripe.
Shakespeare   *Othello*

He learns from his father

The life-giving value of watering the lawn

each blade of grass and each clump of weeds.

Their thirst or his playtime?

He dances the droplets about

glittering in the sunlight while

'funnily' tangling the hose

for funfilled unknotting later!

He learns from his father.

mmc

ANTICIPATION

One of the most attractive things about flowers is their

beautiful reserve. Henry David Thoreau, (1817-1862)

Like a patchwork quilt,

the different patterns of color

create unique sections,

each a delight to behold.

Yet together a wonder

that changes from day to day.

                    Leslie A. Slade, 2007

116

Look deep into nature and then you will understand

everything better.   Albert Einstein, (1879-1955)

120

The last droplets fall from the
delicate dancing faces,
drying in the breezes.

mmc

Nature is sustained by water, earth and light.

She is as seductive as the Greek Sirens

in appearance and

overwhelmingly in fragrance.

mmc

122

Yes as every one knows,

meditation and water

are wedded forever.

Herman Melville, *Moby Dick,* 1851

124

Two displayed in all their glory.

Two the result of hand-watering

and disciplined care

of the single plant.

Two returning their energy

to the single nurturer.

Offspring of love,

bring joy to the soul.

                    mmc

126

Nature's Kaliedoscope never ceases to amaze.

Wet or dry there is glory to behold.   mmc

We have much to hope from the flowers.

Sir Arthur Conan Doyle, (1859-1930)

A globe of dew

Filling, in the morning new,...

On an unimagined world;

Constellated suns unshaken,

Orbits measureless are furl'd

In that frail and fading sphere,

With ten millions gathered there

To tremble, gleam and disappear.

Percy Bysshe Shelley, 1819
Ode to Heaven

Kissing Cousins

Are you going to Scarborough Fair?
Parsley, sage, rosemary, and thyme.... Paul Simon

Hand-watering plants in your garden

with Mother Nature's support

will take you on jouneys

to her special beauties.

And

take you to sense your inner beauty ---

heart, mind and soul.

Keep that passion for watering.

mmc

The morns are meeker than they were,

The nuts are getting brown;

The berry's cheek is plumper,

The rose is out of town.

The maple wears a gayer scarf,

The field a scarlet gown.

Lest I should be old-fashioned,

I'll put a trinket on.

Emily Dickinson, (1830-1886),
Nature 27 - Autumn

CONTRIBUTING PHOTOGRAPHERS

ALL PHOTOGRAPHS ARE BY MATTHEW M. COHEN EXCEPT AS NOTED BELOW. Contributed photographs were cropped to fit the page without consultation of the contributor. The contributing photographers are listed in alphabetical order—last name first, then first name, then (home country), then the page on which the photo(s) can be found, then the (subject by common name or by Genus which will have the first letter capitalized), followed by the copyright year and symbol. These photographers retain the Copyright(s);

Appleby, Janine, (England), pp88&89(crocus), ©2005, p97(thistle), ©2005, Arvola, Kirsi, (Finland), p99(grass with frosted morning dew), ©2006, Brynjúlfsdóttir, Helga, (Iceland), p13(backyard with flower garden), ©2007, p42(allium), Cohen, Gabe, (USA), p40(desert garden), ©2004, p59(autumn maple leaves), ©2003, pp78-79(orange nasturtiums), ©2007, Cohen, Leslie, (USA), p93(sunflowers), ©2007, p109(pears), ©2007, Crouthamel, David, (USA), pp70-71(entrance winter then spring), ©2005 then©2006, p141(bench)©2006, Ferris, Kate, (Scotland), p25(green Helliborus), ©2007, Ihori, Mase, (Japan), p131(blue Scilla), ©2007, Jamieson, Christine, (Australia), p128(wet buds), ©2007, Jeringan, Doug, (USA), p69(walking iris), ©2007, Kahn, Zahid, (England), p48(bluebells), ©2007, Kleiner, Lenore, (USA), p111(watering lawn), ©2006, Lamothe, Fleur-Ange, (Canada), p98(translucent poplar leaves), ©2006, McCall, Mary Charlotte, (USA), pp38 &39(brook), ©2006, Russell-Smith, Alicia, (USA), p123(gardenia), ©2007, Schencke, Jutta, (Austria), p77(tulips), ©2006, p95(poppy field), ©2007, p133(dandelion), ©2007, Shternshus, Haim, (USA), p26(lantana and), ©2005, p35(bamboo pump), ©2005, Shternshus, Jessie, (USA), p66(amaryllis), ©2007, p144(water lilly), ©2005, van Deemter, Rita, (Netherlands), p129(prickly leaves), ©2006, p139 (passion flower), ©2006, Yamamoto, Anzu, (Japan), p108 (cherries), ©2005

CONTRIBUTING AUTHORS

ALL APHORISMS AND POEMS ARE BY MATTHEW M. COHEN (mmc), Copyright ©2007: EXCEPT AS NOTED IN THE TEXT AND BY THE AUTHORS BELOW. The contributing authors are listed in alphabetical order—last name first, then first name, then the page on which their aphorism or poem can be found followed by the copyright year. To save space the word copyright has been omitted in the list as discussed above. These authors retain the copyright(s); Blackman, Rachel F., p48, ©2007, Cohen, Stanley L., p100, ©2007, Slade, Leslie A., pp 46 and 116, ©2007.

ACKNOWLEDGEMENTS

I would like to thank my wife, who shared the experience of viewing and photographing gardens here, around the country and abroad. We collectively developed critical eyes for capturing the essence of these experiences. She provided ongoing encouragement and critique of the aesthetics contained in this work.
My friend , Mark, helped me formulate a plan for this book, in many brainstorming sessions. I would like to thank the many people locally, who allowed me carte blanche access to water their plants and then take pictures in their yards whenever there was a cloudy sky or high haze. My, friend, 'MC' helped to encourage my ardent belief in the value of the premise on which this book is based. The internet has made the world a smaller place. A database of 130,000,000 photos posted by many thousands of individuals in thousands of groups with similar interests known as Flickr has reminded me that most people are kind and generous with their time, their thoughts, and their photos. Quite a number of my Flickr "pen/photo" friends offered me access to review well over 5,000 photos of which I chose only a few. But, I am optimistic that this book will be a success and bring them opportunities for publication in future works of mine, or for that matter of their own. Thank you, Friends.

PLANT COMMON NAME & LOCATION IF IN USA
FOLLOWED BY STATE ABBREVIATION.
IF NOT THEN BY COUNTRY.

Cover, Japanese Magnolia, FL
Title Page, Camilla, FL
Dedication, Red Dogwood, FL
13, Backyard Garden, Iceland
15, Japanese Maple, FL
16, 17 Black Eyed Susan, FL
19, 21 Quince, FL
23, Multipetal Daffodil, FL
25, green Helleboe, Scotland
26, 27, Lantana, FL
29, Pine Bark, FL
30, Lichens, FL
32,33, Japanese Cherry, FL
37, Cactus, FL
38,39, Brook with moss, AK
40, Cactus, Israel
41, Cactus Garden, CA
42, Alliums, Iceland
43, purple Petunia, FL
44, 45, salmon pink Azalea, FL
47, 'elephant tree', Spain
48, Bluebells, England
49, Roses, FL
51, purple flowers, FL
53, Lotus bud & glass floats, NY
55, yellow flowers tree, FL
56.57 Water Garden, FL
59, Red Maple, NC
60, Nasturtiums, AK
61, Nasturtiums, CA
63, dark purple flowers, Fl
65 Shrimp Plant, FL
66, 67, red Amaryllis, FL
69 Walking Iris, FL
71, 72 Store Entrance, ME
73, Zucchini, CA
74, Tomatoes, AK
75, Bonsai Juniper on Driftwood, CA
77, very wet Tulips, Austria
78, 79, orange multipetaled Poppies, NY

81, Sycamore, FL
83, Plant in Planter, Spain
84, Flame Tree, Poinciana, Israel
85, Powder Puff Mimosa, FL
86, 87, Garden, CA
88, 89, Crocus, England
90, 91, Planter, Persian Shield, CT
93, Sunflowers, FL
94, Poppies, Turkey
95, Poppy field, Austria
97, Thistle, England
98, Poplar leaves dripping, Canada
99, Grass frozen dew, Finland
101, Gerbera Daises, FL
103, Stone Pagoda, Ferns, FL
104,105 Miniature Kalanchoes, FL
107, Weeping Bald Cypress, FL
108, Cherries, Japan
109, Pears, CA
111, Child Watering,
112,113 purple Azalea, FL
114, white Wisteria, FL
115, white Poppy, White Kale, FL
117, Front Yard Garden, CA
118,119, Spider Lily, FL
120,121, Pansies, FL
123, Gardenia, MA
125, Koi Pond & leaves
127, Cattleya Orchid, FL
128, wet Geraldton buds, Australia
129, prickly leaves Netherlands
130, blue African Violet, FL
131, blue flowers, Japan
133, Dandelion, Austria
134,135, Kangaroo-Paws, CA
136, Herb Garden, FL
137, Parsley, FL
139, Passion Flower, Netherlands
141, Fallen Leaves, ME
145, Water Lilly, NC
BOTANICAL NAMES AVAILABLE ON WWW.
ZENOFWATERING.COM

Further information about
Zen of Watering™ *Your Garden* and
botanical plant names can be
found at www.zenofwatering.com

Information about other Zen of Watering™
products is available at www.zofw.com

This book is published by the
Sunbelt Publishers Division
www.sunbeltpublishers.com

of Sunbelt Medical Publishers, Inc.
P. O. Box 13512,
Tallahassee, Fl 32317-13512
www.sunbeltmed.com

Please Direct inquiries to the
Sunbelt Publishers Division
www.sunbeltpublishers.com